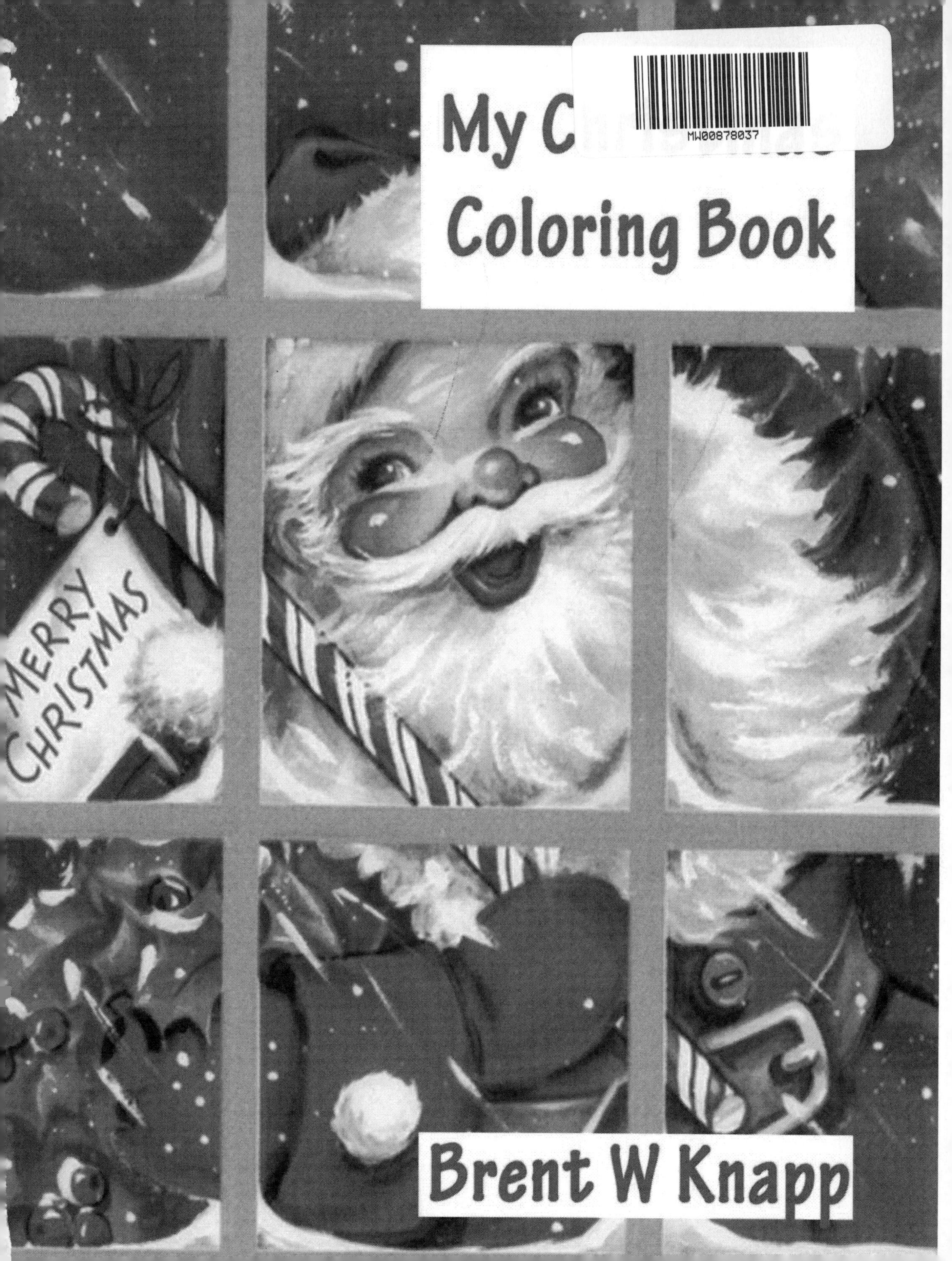


# My C
# Coloring Book



Brent W Knapp

**Copyright Information**



Published by: Iconic Animation, Inc.

ISBN: 1-4515533-1-5

Email: info@iconicanimation.com

Manufactured in the United States of America

10 9 8 7 6 5 4 3 2 1

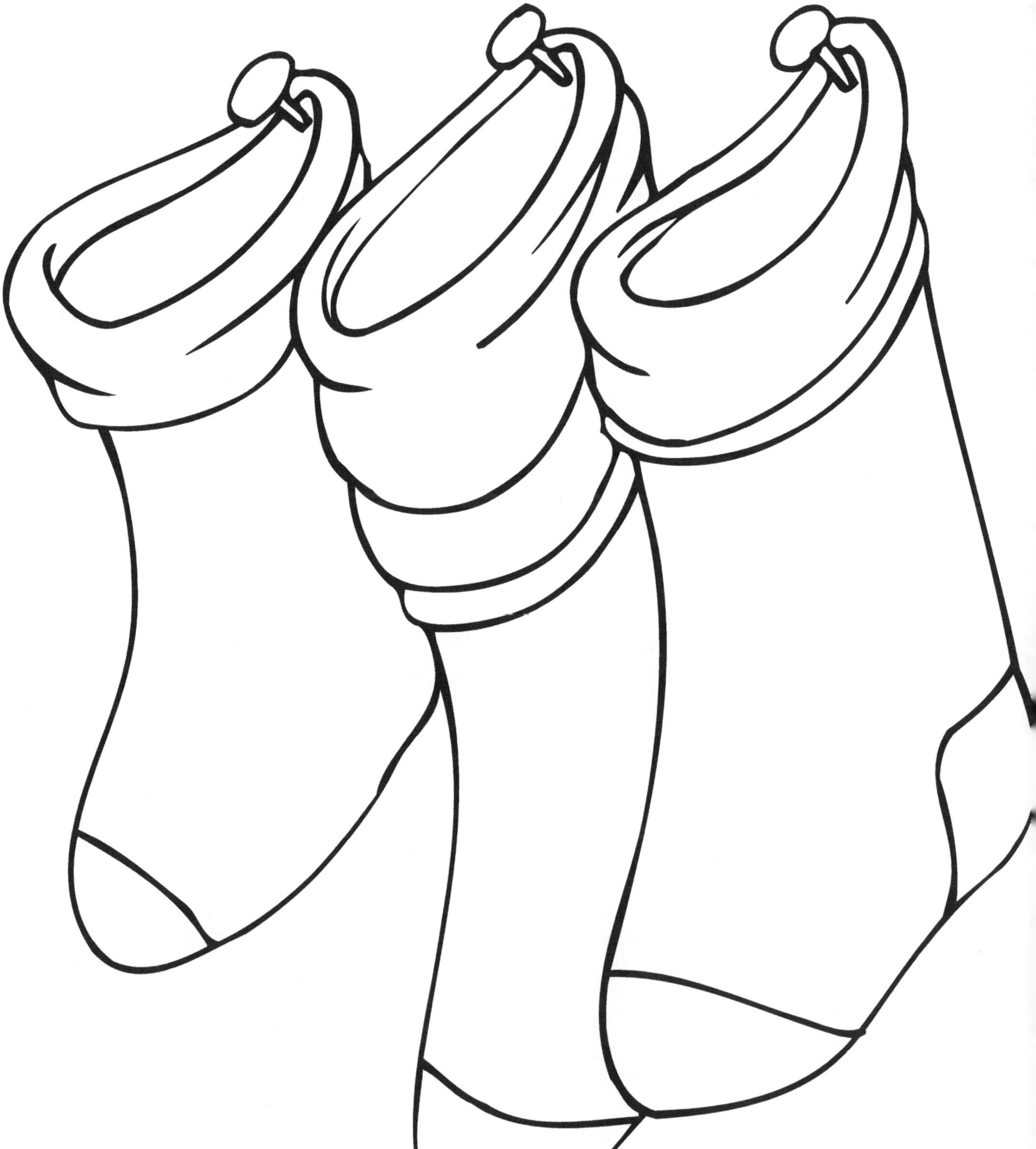

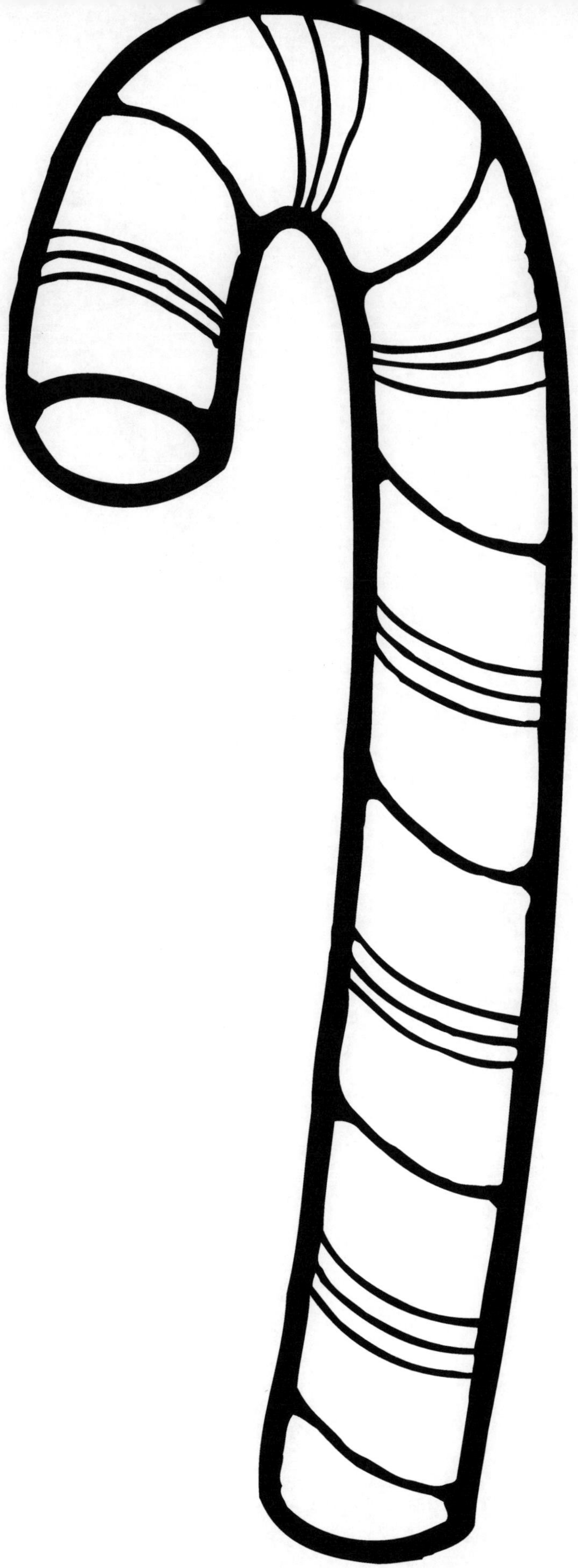

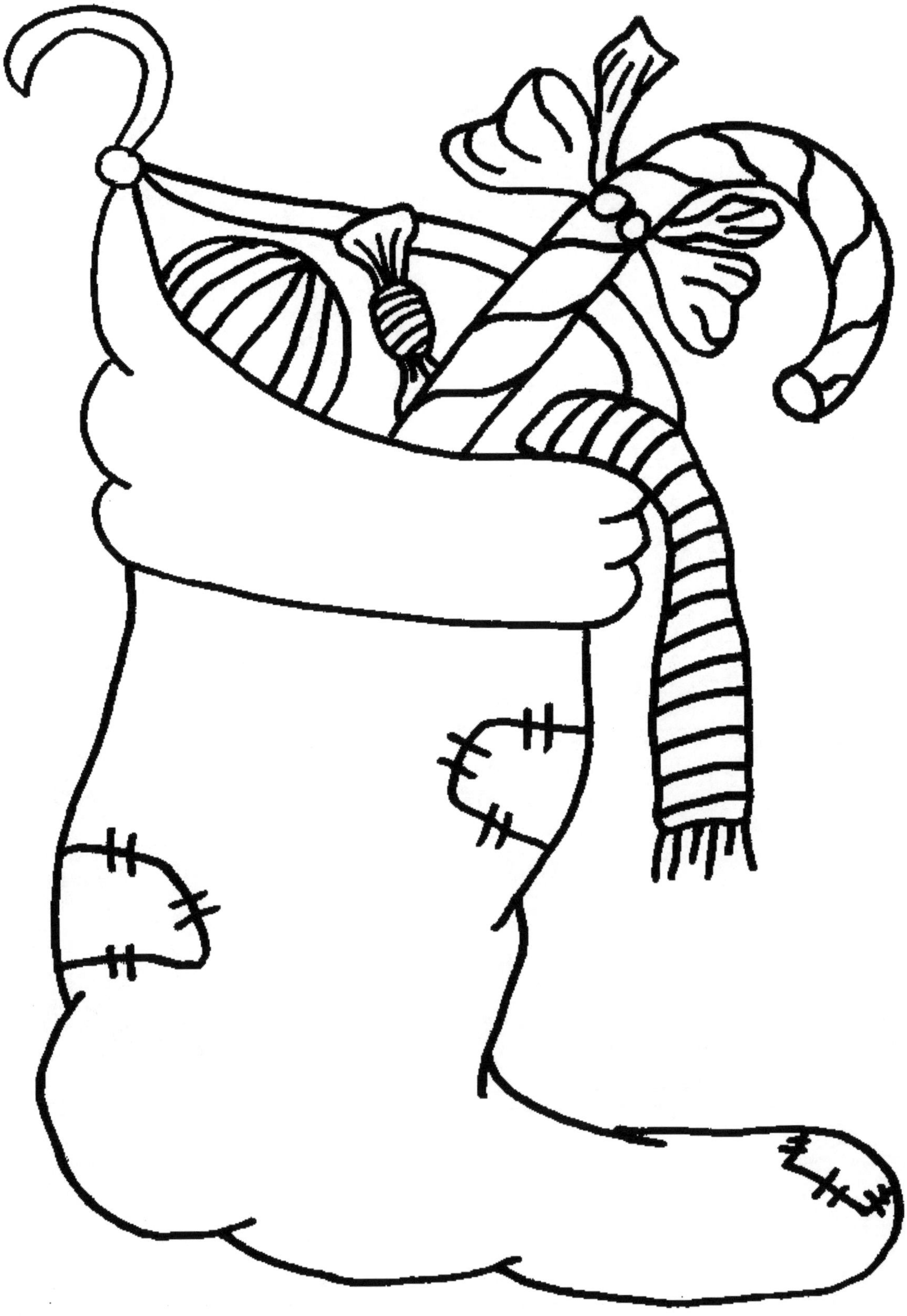

Merry Christmas!

TO
FROM

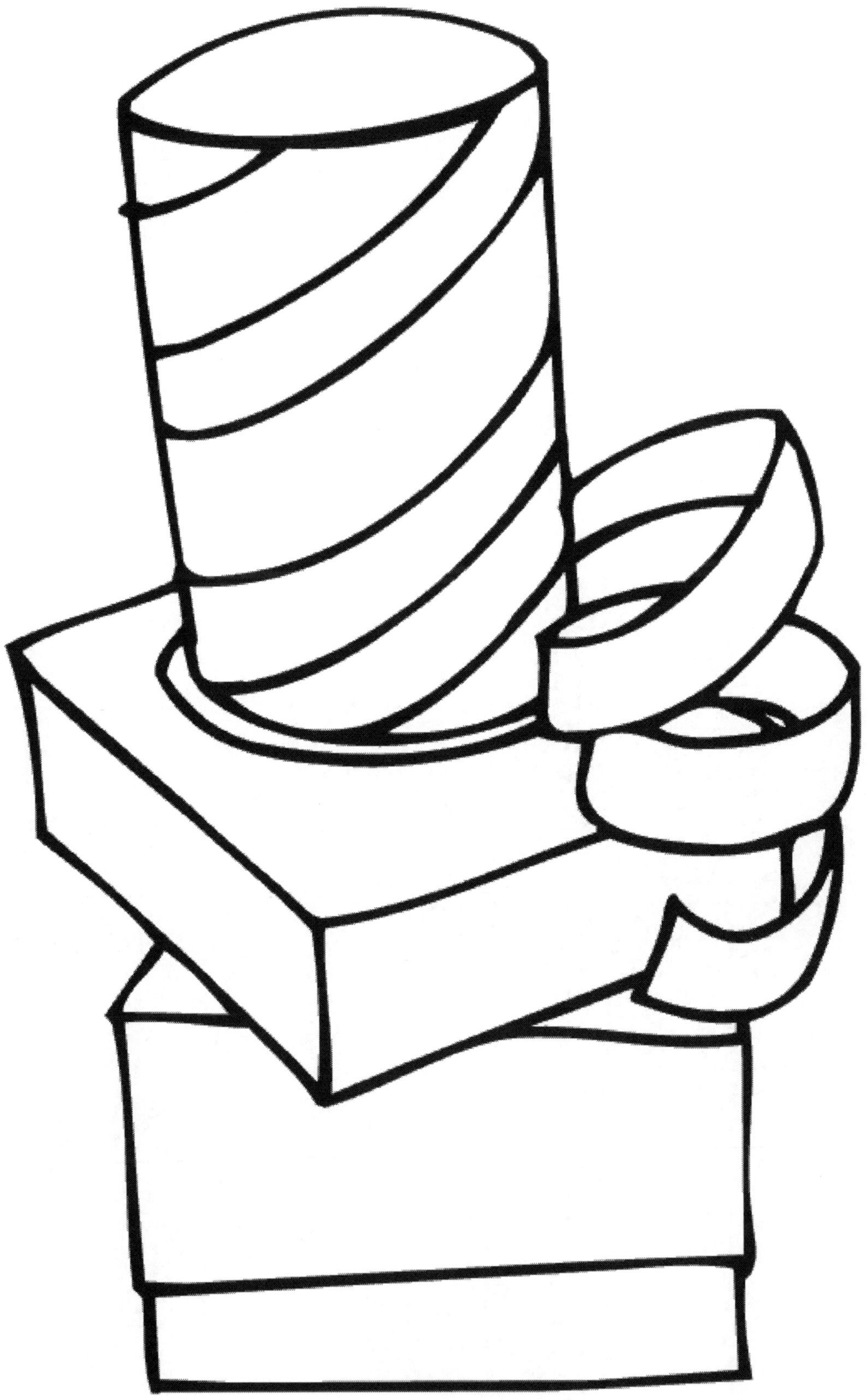

There's Snowflake Like Home!

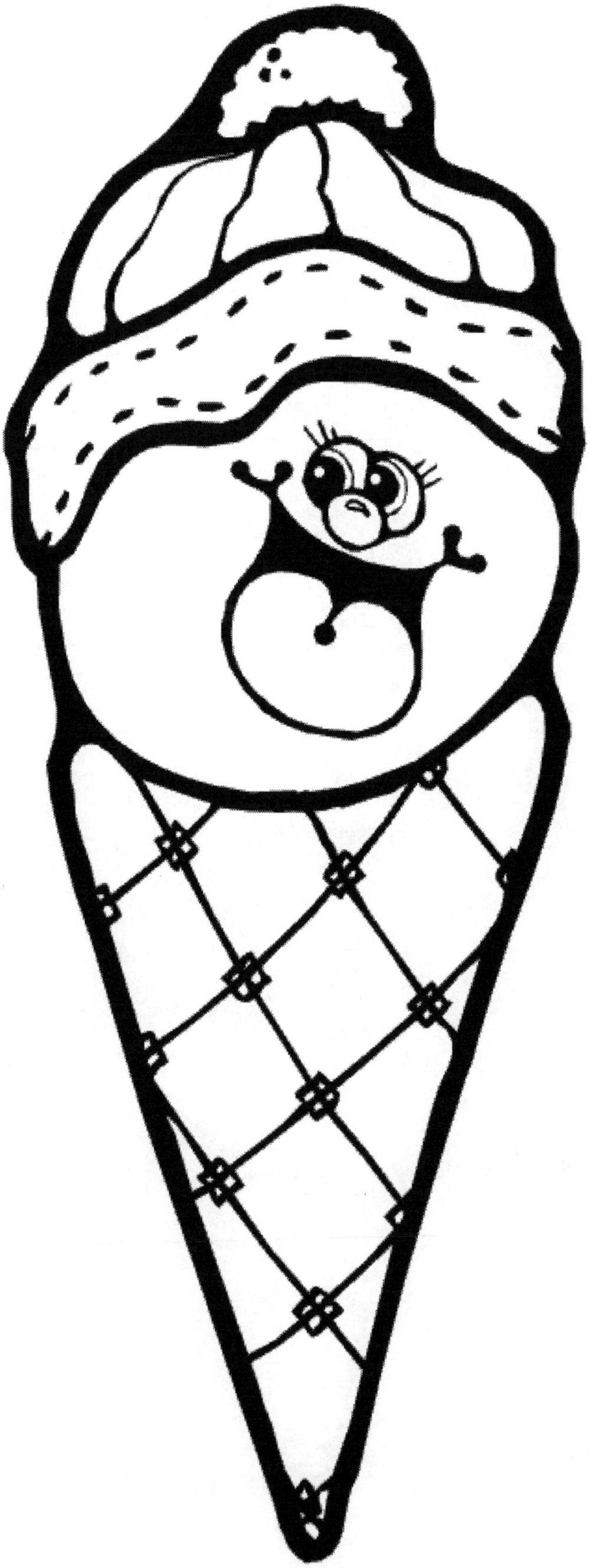

Merry Christmas

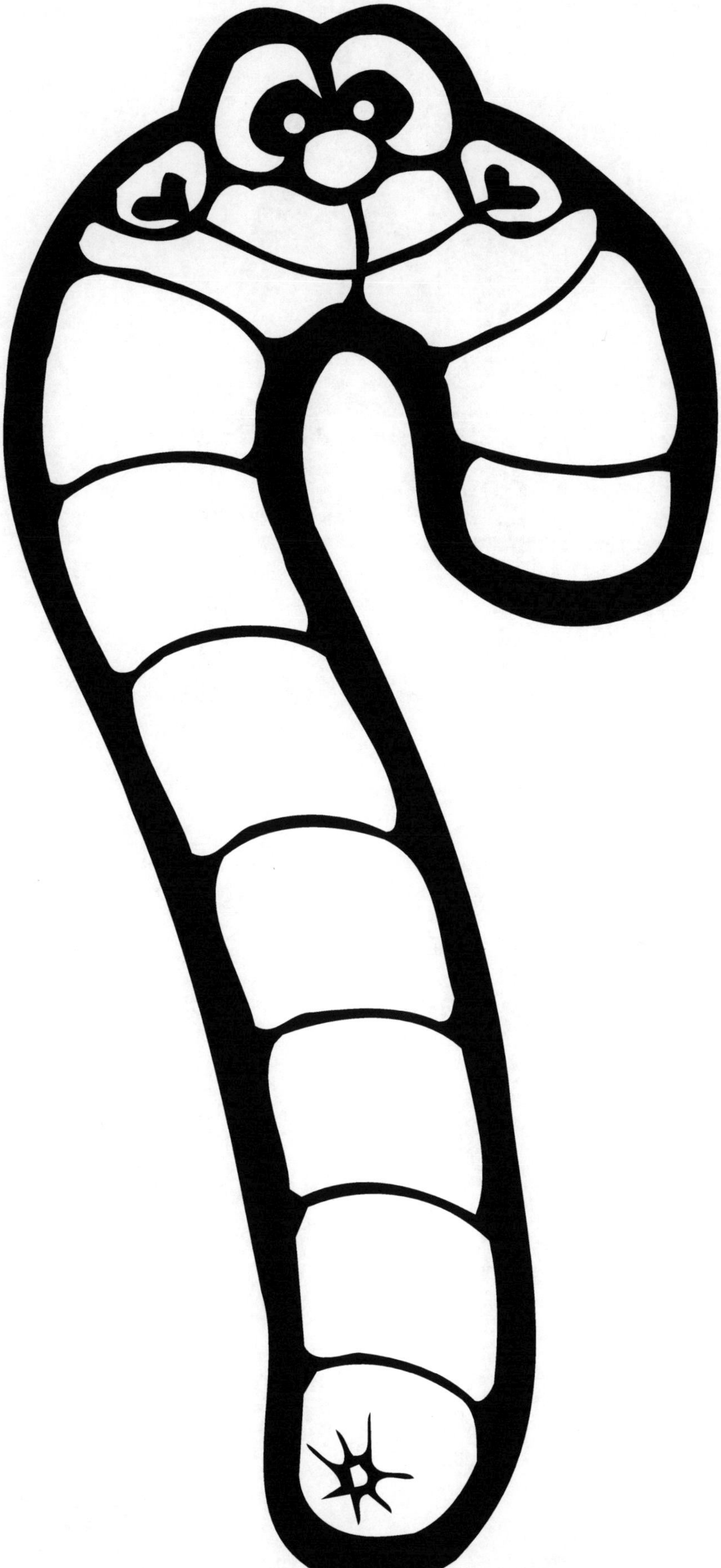

N

95611272R00053

Made in the USA
Middletown, DE
28 October 2018